WRESTLING

A TRUE BOOK

by

Christin Ditchfield

Children's Press®

A Division of Grolier Publishing

New York London Hong Kong Sydney
Danbury, Connecticut

An Olympic Greco-Roman wrestling match

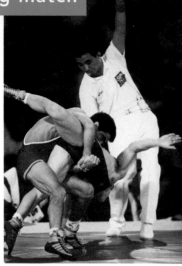

Reading Consultant
Linda Cornwell
Coordinator of School Quality
and Professional Improvement
Indiana State Teachers
Association

Photo Consultant
Lou Montano
Head Wrestling Coach
Columbia University, New York

The photograph on the cover shows a Greco-Roman wrestling match. The photo on the title page shows an overhead view of a wrestling match.

Visit Children's Press® on
the Internet at:
http://publishing.grolier.com

Library of Congress Cataloging-in-Publication Data

Ditchfield, Christin.
  Wrestling / by Christin Ditchfield.
     p.   cm. — (a true book)
  Includes bibliographical references (p.) and index.
  Summary: Describes the history, rules, and styles of wrestling.
  ISBN 0-516-21611-2 (lib. bdg.)   0-516-27033-8 (pbk.)
  1. Wrestling Juvenile literature. [1. Wrestling.] I. Title. II. Series.
GV1195.3.D58 2000
796,812—dc21   99-28191
                                                                    CIP
                                                                    AC

GROLIER
PUBLISHING

Contents

Wrestling is one of the world's oldest sports.

Long Ago

Wrestling is one of the oldest and simplest sports in the world. The athletes compete against each other without any weapons or special equipment. They use only their own strength and skill.

In the beginning, people wrestled for fun and exercise.

Soldiers wrestled to keep fit for battle. Sometimes a wrestling match was used to settle an argument between two men. Wrestlers competed in the ancient Olympics and other special competitions.

Wrestling had very few rules in the early days, so a wrestling match could be brutal. Opponents kicked, slapped, and bit each other. The match ended when one of the competitors surrendered—or died.

In the early days of wrestling, there were few rules and matches could be brutal.

Today, there are two kinds of wrestling—amateur and professional. Professional wrestling is more entertainment than sport. The competitors wrestle violently and dramatically—and leave the audience to wonder how real it all is.

This book is about amateur wrestling, which is a true competitive sport. Amateur wrestlers follow a strict code of conduct. Rules make the

Amateur wrestling is an exciting sport to watch.

matches fair and safe for everyone. But amateur wrestling is still one of the most exciting sports to watch!

The Basics

In competitive wrestling, the object is to throw the opponent on his back so that both of his shoulder blades touch the ground at the same time. To do this, wrestlers use special moves that involve throwing, twisting, lifting, or tackling the competitor.

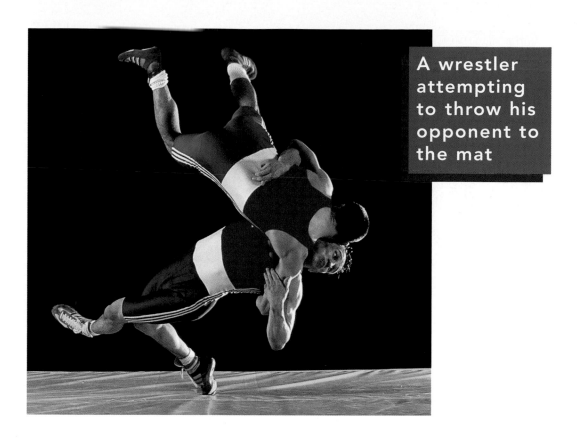

It's important for a wrestler to be strong, but quickness and physical fitness are even more important. Wrestlers rely on skill and technique more than on strength.

Wrestlers wear a one-piece uniform called a singlet.

Wrestlers wear short, tight outfits called singlets. Special shoes give the athletes extra ankle support. Before the match, each wrestler is weighed. He will compete against other athletes in the same weight class. International competitive wrestling has eight official weight classes, each with its own name and weight limit. These classes range from "light fly-weight" to "superheavyweight."

A wrestler weighing in before a match

Many high schools and colleges have wrestling programs. At the high-school and college level, there are state, district, national, and international competitions.

High-school wrestlers

The wrestlers try to stay within the circular line drawn around the competition area.

A wrestling match takes place on a large padded mat with a 29.5-foot (9-m) circular competition area. At the start

of a match, the competitors stand facing each other inside the center ring.

A referee watches the match closely. He awards points for various holds and moves. A

The referee awards points and keeps the match safe.

judge confirms the referee's call and puts the points on the scoreboard. If the judge and the referee disagree, the match-chairman makes the final decision.

International wrestling matches are 6 minutes long. If no points have been scored at the end of the 6 minutes, the timekeeper may signal for 3 minutes of overtime.

A match automatically ends when one of the competitors holds the opponent's shoulder blades to the mat for 1/2 second, or when one of the athletes is ahead by ten points.

Collegiate wrestling bouts are 7 minutes long, and high-school bouts are 6 minutes long. In both collegiate and high-school wrestling, the match is over when one wrestler holds the opponent's shoulders to the mat for 1 second.

Wrestling Styles

The two basic types of wrestling are freestyle and Greco-Roman. In both styles, wrestlers use similar moves and techniques to pin their opponents to the mat. But in Greco-Roman wrestling, the competitors attack and hold each other with the arms and

Only the arms and upper body can be used in Greco-Roman wrestling.

Freestyle wrestlers can use both arms and legs to execute holds or defend against attack.

upper body only. Freestyle wrestling allows the athletes to use their legs too.

A wrestler wins points for a takedown—when he forces his

A takedown

opponent down on the mat. Points are also given for exposures and reversals. An exposure involves turning an opponent's shoulders to the

The wrestler in red is attempting a reversal.

mat. A reversal takes place when the athlete who is underneath his opponent manages to come out on top.
Wrestlers lose points for fouls—illegal moves. Fouls

include tripping an opponent, stepping on his feet, or gripping his throat. The athletes must not speak to each other during the match.

Gripping an opponent's throat is a foul.

At the Olympics

Wrestling has always been an important part of the Olympic Games. In the modern games, athletes compete for medals in each weight class in both freestyle and Greco-Roman events.

Some of the greatest Olympic wrestlers have come

A wrestling match during the 1908 London Olympics

An Olympic
Greco-Roman
match between
wrestlers from
Turkey and
Germany

from countries where the sport
is extremely popular, such as
Japan, Turkey, and Iran.
However, Russia and the
United States lead the medal

counts. Russians have domi-
nated the Greco-Roman
events, while Americans hold
the most freestyle medals.

An American and a Russian wrestler
battling it out during an Olympic heavy-
weight Greco-Roman wrestling final

The Olympics have several rounds of wrestling competition. All of the winners in the first round go into the "A draw." These wrestlers compete against one another for the gold (first-place) and silver (second-place) medals. The losers from the first round compete in the "B draw." The winner of this group receives the bronze (third-place) medal.

The Champions

Over the years, there have been many great wrestling champions. Alexander Medwed, competing for the Soviet Union in the Greco-Roman competition, won three consecutive Olympic gold medals in 1964, 1968, and 1972. Medwed was crowned

world champion seven times
and captured the European
Championships three times.
Many American wrestlers
have won freestyle medals,

but Steve Fraser was the first American to win gold in a Greco-Roman event. He earned his medal at the 1984 Los Angeles Olympics.

Steve Fraser (in red)

Bruce Baumgartner during a match (above) and after winning a match (left)

Bruce Baumgartner will probably go down in history as the most successful international wrestler ever. He won many prestigious wrestling competitions, including three World Championships. But the most incredible achievement of his career is his Olympic record. Baumgartner won medals in four different Olympics, from 1984 to 1996. He captured two gold medals, a silver, and a bronze.

Women's Wrestling

Tricia Saunders (in red), the 1999 Women's U.S. Nationals champion

Wrestling isn't just for men anymore. Women have begun competing in freestyle events at junior and world championship levels. At first, women who wanted to wrestle had to compete in special clubs or on men's teams.

The University of Minnesota-Morris
was the first college to open a varsity
wrestling program just for women. Now
several countries have
national women's
teams.

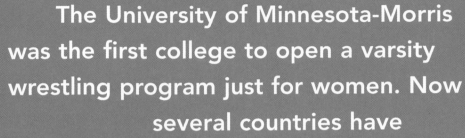

A collegiate
women's
wrestling
match

Other Wrestling Sports

Any sport that involves hand-to-hand combat without weapons can be called wrestling. Karate, judo, and other martial arts may sometimes be considered wrestling sports.

Another type of wrestling is sumo wrestling—the national

Women's judo

sport of Japan. Sumo matches take place in a 15-foot (4.5-m) ring built on a low platform.

Sumo wrestling is the national sport of Japan.

The wrestlers try to force their opponents out of the ring. They may push, pull, slap, throw, or trip their competitors. As soon as the other wrestler steps or stumbles out of the ring, the match is over.

Sumo wrestlers must weigh at least 150 pounds (67.5 kg), and many weigh more than

Japanese sumo wrestler Yasukichi Konishiki

300 pounds (135 kg). These wrestlers use their size to help them out-muscle their opponents. Sumo wrestlers compete wearing special belts called *mawashis.*

Sumo wrestling is so popular all over Asia that the champions become celebrities. Crowds follow these wrestling superstars everywhere. But in Western countries, few people are interested in sumo wrestling—and even fewer

Sumo wrestling is very popular in Asia.

compete. In the 1980s, American Jesse Kahualua became the first sumo champion from a non-Asian country.

To Find Out More

Here are some additional resources to help you learn more about wrestling:

 **Books**

Gutman, Bill. **Sumo Wrestling.** Capstone Press, 1995.

Ledeboer, Suzanne. **A Basic Guide to Wrestling.** USOC, 1997.

Savage, Jeff. **Wrestling Basics.** Capstone Press, 1996.

Thomas, Ron and Joe Herran. **The Grolier Student Encyclopedia of the Olympic Games.** Grolier Educational, 1996.

Wallechinsky, David. **The Complete Book of the Summer Olympics.** Little, Brown & Co., 1996.

☀ Organizations and Online Sites

The Mat—Home of Amateur Wrestling
http://www.themat.com

Provides all the latest news about amateur wrestling.

United States Olympic Committee (USOC) Olympic House
One Olympic Plaza
Colorado Springs, CO
80909-5760
http://www.usoc.org

The United States Olympic Committee supervises Olympic activity for the United States. Its website includes everything you want to know about Olympic sports, past and present.

USA Wrestling
6155 Lehman Drive
Colorado Springs, CO
80918
http://www.usawrestling.org

This is the national governing body for amateur wrestling in the United States. It coordinates wrestling programs across the country and works to create interest and participation in wrestling. Its members include athletes, coaches, parents, and fans.

Important Words

bout contest between two wrestlers; match

class weight group

collegiate at the college level

execute carry out, do

mawashi loincloth or belt worn by sumo wrestlers

pin act of holding an opponent's shoulders to the mat for at least one-half of a second; also known as a "fall"

reversal changing the position from one of disadvantage to advantage

singlet one-piece uniform worn by wrestlers

surrendered gave up

takedown act of taking one's opponent to the mat from a standing position

Index

(**Boldface** page numbers
indicate illustrations.)

Meet the Author

Christin Ditchfield is the author of several books for Children's Press, including five True Books on Summer Olympic sports. Her interviews with celebrity athletes have appeared in magazines all over the world. Ms. Ditchfield makes her home in Sarasota, Florida.